Kidege

Life Through the Eyes of a Kenyan Youth

Aaron Arnold

Jesse Frame

Dale Puckett

Kidege
Life Through the Eyes
of a Kenyan Youth

ISBN-13: 978-1544198552
ISBN-10: 1544198558

General Editor
Jesse Frame

Content Consultant
Phil Hudson

Cover art by Solly Smook
Cover design by Drew McClary

*This book is dedicated to girls like Ruth
who face and conquer challenges
bigger that we can often comprehend*

and

*to all the men and women
who are working to transform the lives
of youth around the world.*

*Youth are our greatest hope
for a better future.*

youthH★PE
transforming lives of global youth

This book was written and published
by members of the YouthHOPE team.
YouthHOPE exists to transform the lives of global youth
by equipping the church to meet their holistic needs.
youthhope.com

YouthHOPE works in partnership with...

Ends of the Earth Cycling exists to promote and resource
global youth ministry through prayer, awareness,
fundraising and a whole lot of FUN!
endscycling.com

AfricaHope

AfricaHope ministers to youth like those depicted in the
book using Truth and Hope to Transform lives.
africahope.org

YouthHOPE, Ends of the Earth Cycling, and AfricaHope
are ministries of New Mission Systems International.
nmsi.org

cover art by

Solly Smook

sollysmook.com

Special thanks to Solly Smook for allowing
YouthHOPE's designer, Drew McClary, to use
his beautiful painting for the cover of *Kidege*.

Table of Contents

PREFACE

You are reading this book because, in some way, you care about young people. For that reason, you are an awesome person! You are also in good company. You are joining a movement around the world focused on intentionally investing in the lives of youth and adolescents. Youth ages 12-24 make up nearly 25% of the people living on this planet. That totals 1.8 billion youth, a number possibly unfathomable. It's close to double the population of China, the world's largest country. So in other words, there is a super-massive amount of youth. Another fact you should know is most of them live in less developed countries where they face significant challenges. Access to healthcare, access to education, lack of safety, unemployment, religious persecution, gender discrimination, and extreme poverty are just a few of the issues most of the world's youth face. There is no doubt those numbers and the realities youth face are just plain overwhelming. What could you do? Where could you start? Could you make a difference?

The purpose of this book is to help you think through and begin to answer those questions. The first part of each chapter is an episode in the story of a young person from Kenya. Ruth is a 14-year-old girl. Her story is based on culture, statistical data, and personal experiences. Ruth represents the reality mentioned above but she is not a real person. As you read about her life, her struggles, her heroes, and her accomplishments, you will get a small idea of what it is like to walk in her shoes. As you read her story you will be accomplishing the first goal of this book which is to EMPATHIZE with global youth and the circumstances in which they live.

The second part of each chapter highlights one of the issues Ruth is facing in her life as a youth growing up in Kenya. There are seven issues we address:
1.   Education
2.   Family
3.   Identity
4.   Safety
5.   Injustice
6.   Voice
7.   Faith

As you read more about these issues and interact with statistics, facts, and figures, you will be accomplishing the second goal of this book; you will LEARN about the reality of a global youth. This new information, we hope, will inspire you to action.

At the end of each chapter, there will be a set of questions that will help you process what you've read. This can be done alone or with a group of people who are reading the book together. By the way, this story was written in a way that it can easily be read aloud with your small group, family, or Sunday School class. By answering the questions, you will be accomplishing the third goal of the book which is to REFLECT. It's important to take some time and think about what you have learned and how this makes you feel. So, don't skip the questions! At least take some time to think through them, even if you don't take time to write down any of your answers.

Ruth is waiting for you on the next page! As you read her story, don't hesitate to close your eyes and imagine the scene, what the characters look like, or the emotions they are experiencing. This is a story which brings to light some very tough issues many girls in Kenya and other parts of the world face. While the story reveals some of the ugliness of man and sin, it also highlights that God has a plan for global youth, plans to prosper them, not to harm them, to give them hope and a future.

CHAPTER ONE

Education

"RUTH, GET UP NOW!" yelled her mom from outside where she was finishing cooking food for the family. Usually, Sundays were a day to sleep in and relax, whether she was here at home or at her boarding school. However, this was not the case today because Christmas break was over and Ruth was going back to school right after church was over. It was about two hours from her village in southwestern Kenya and really the only chance she had for a good education.

She had enjoyed her last few weeks at home with the family. Her mom, Namelok[1], was a beautiful and caring woman. Ruth always felt loved and special when she was around her and she encouraged Ruth to continue her studies. Her mom had stopped going to school after primary school because that's just what girls did when she was growing up. She wanted more for her daughter and many times had fought with her husband, John, about investing in their daughter's education and future. It wasn't that

---

[1] Pronounced NAM-EH-LOK. In Maasai, it means "the sweet one."

he didn't love his daughter, but he was a traditional and practical man. He worked hard both at his job changing tires on the lorries that broke down on the highway near their village and with his cattle herding. He saw education as a luxury and didn't have much hope that a daughter was worth investing that much money in. He had a hard time seeing beyond the place of a woman being something other than a wife or mother. However, she had done so well and achieved such high marks that he could not say no, at least for now.

Ruth closed her eyes and sang as loud as she could. It was going to be her last chance for a few months to be at her church here in the village. Though it was small and most of the people were older, she felt a peace that was hard to explain. She had come to church with her mother since she was a little girl. First, it was just the two of them, but now her younger brothers and sister also went. She loved to see them sing and dance before running off with their Sunday School teacher to have their class under the acacia tree just outside the church building. She wished her dad would come with them, but he was always busy working or many times Sunday was the day he met with the other village elders to discuss important issues or resolve some conflict. He was a respected man and that made her proud. However, it always seemed like he wasn't happy and she wondered if it had anything to do with him not having the hope she found in Jesus. She always invited him every Sunday and she planned to keep on doing it.

"Why don't you have your things ready, Ruth? We have to walk to the highway soon or you will miss the bus when it passes by. Hurry up!" said Ruth's mom. Ruth stuffed her last few white shirts, that were part of her school uniform, into her duffel bag.

"Back to boring clothes," she thought to herself, as she was not the biggest fan of the uniforms she had to wear every day at her boarding school. It could be worse, though. She could be stuck in her village like many of the girls she grew up with. Some of them were already getting married. Ruth took just a moment and thought about what that would be like. She was 14 years old, well almost 15 as her birthday was coming up before the semester ended. Married? And most of the girls she knew were married to old men. That made her stomach hurt.

"Focus daughter!" sternly chided her mother, "you are staring off into the sky. Zip up your bag and let's go."

It was about a 30-minute walk to the highway, the one her father took every day to go to work. She held one side of her duffel bag and her mother held the other while carrying her youngest brother, Jacob, on her back. She was going to miss him. She had lots of fun with him during her break, as he was just starting to run around and play. He was almost too big to be carried around like her mom was doing, but it was the only way to keep him out of trouble on the walk.

As they stood there waiting, she glanced over at her mother. She looked tired and maybe a little bit sad.

"Are you alright, yeyo[2]?" Ruth asked.

Namelok smiled and took her daughter's face in her hands and said, "Don't you worry about me. You go to school. You study hard. God has a plan for you."

Before the tear could roll all the way down her cheek, Ruth heard the blaring horn of the bus, calling out to potential passengers that it was slowing down and they needed to be ready to jump on board. Ruth violently hugged her mother, kissed Jacob on the cheek and pushed her way onto the bus. She hoped to find a seat for the two-hour ride. More than likely, she would be standing.

Ruth woke up startled as she felt someone trying to take her duffel bag from her. She noticed because she had hooked one of the straps through her arms. It was hot and she had not been able to keep her eyes open. Being alone on the bus ride, this was her only security measure. She looked up from her seat to see who it was that was trying to steal her bag. Immediately she saw Kingasunye[3], who was laughing uncontrollably.

"That's not funny!" Ruth shouted.

"You should have seen your face! I wish I had taken a photo, but my mobile battery is dead." Kingasunye was one of Ruth's best friends from school. She must have gotten on the bus while Ruth

---

[2] Pronounced YEE-YOH. In Maasai, it means "mother."
[3] Pronounced KING-A-SOON-YAY. In Maasai, it means "chubby/fat."

was sleeping and took advantage of it to play a joke on her. This was nothing new, as Kingasunye was known for that at school. In fact, she got in pretty serious trouble with the headmaster last semester for a prank that she pulled. Ruth loved her, though. She was always there for Ruth and helped her with English homework, which was Ruth's worst subject. Their beds were next to each other and they would sometimes whisper late into the night talking about going to university and how they were going to be successful Kenyan women.

For the rest of the trip to school, Kingasunye and Ruth caught each other up on what had happened during Christmas break. Both of them had a very good time with their families and both were ready to get back to school. The bus came to a quick stop as it entered the town where the Nala Girls Academy was located. The streets were busy with people going to market to buy and sell. Ruth and Kingasunye got off the bus and pushed their way through the crowds to make it back to the school before they missed dinner.

CRITICAL ISSUE: EDUCATION

Imagine you're in Kenya. You live in a small village many miles from the nearest town. You are 14 years old and you love school. But like Ruth, there are barriers to getting an education. An obstacle course of environmental, financial, social, and cultural hurdles stands in your way. How many miles would you walk? How long would you stay away from home? What if you could not afford the school fees? What if your parents and even your community told you to stay home? What if the plan for your life was being written by someone else? Ruth represents the real young people throughout Kenya who must answer these hard questions.

There are more than 70 million adolescents not enrolled in school around the world. More than 20 million of them live in Sub-Saharan Africa. Tens of thousands of these adolescents live throughout Kenya. Educational numbers are the worst among the poor and among girls.

The question is, "What difference does education make in the life of a poor Kenyan girl?"

Education is a key that can open the door to a transformed life. For girls in Kenya, like Ruth, education helps eliminate poverty. Every year of secondary school education has the potential to increase a girl's future income by 10-20%. Education promotes gender equality. It helps girls like Ruth avoid the dangers of early marriage, sexual abuse, and human trafficking. Education fosters more peaceful societies through tolerance and understanding.

For a girl like Ruth, access to education can mean all the difference. She could stay in her village, marry at age 14, and get pregnant by a much older man. Like so many others, she could then die giving birth.

Alternatively, she could continue her schooling. This not only increases her potential to earn a living wage but also gives her the confidence to try. She could then afford basic health care, eat a healthier diet, contribute to her community, and literally make Kenya a better place. She and her future family could be one big step out of the cycle of poverty.

Ruth deserves an education not because she shows potential as a good student, but because every girl should have the opportunity to gain knowledge, learn new skills, scale the walls of poverty, and contribute to making the world a better place.

Education is praised throughout the bible. In fact, we're told in various ways that an education is more valuable than material things.[4] God has preserved entire volumes in order that we may gain wisdom, instruction, understanding, knowledge, and guidance.[5] God used educated, intelligent young

[4] Proverbs 16:16
[5] Proverbs 1:2–5

men like Daniel[6] to accomplish great things at the highest levels of society. The gospel writer Luke tells us that even Jesus had to grow in wisdom and stature[7].

Opportunity is a priceless commodity. While we may take our educational opportunities for granted, there are millions of young people around the world who are desperate for a different life afforded by education. The Church must continue to promote education and create educational opportunities for youth.

[6] Daniel 1:17
[7] Luke 2:52

QUESTIONS

1. Think about being 14 years old and having the opportunity to receive a valuable education at a boarding school. As excited as you might be to attend school, what would you miss about your family, your home, and your town/city?

2. How do you think a girl like Ruth would feel knowing her mother supported her education but her father did not see it as important?

3. How has your education (or lack of education) been a factor in your life?

4. What fact about education in this chapter stood out to you the most? Why?

5. How do you feel knowing that so many young people, especially girls, face barriers to receiving an education?

CHAPTER TWO

Family

Buzz...buzz...buzz vibrated Ruth's phone. She panicked a little as they were in the middle of their first quiz of the semester. It was math class and while it is one of her best subjects, she still needed to concentrate. Mr. Hamaki[8], her math teacher, was very strict and demanding. He allowed no funny business and receiving text messages was something he did not tolerate. She hoped whoever it was would stop texting her—at least until after this class ended. She was curious as she didn't really receive too many messages at school, expect from her mom and it was usually in the evening before going to bed. Ruth closed her eyes and then opened them, trying to focus all of her attention on the math problems that were left on her quiz.

---

[8] Pronounced HA-MA-KEE. In Swahili, it means "angry."

"mother is sick. u must come home 2 work here"
"call me tonight after my work"

She read the text messages from her father again, for the tenth time. It had been less than one month since she left home and as far as she knew, her mother was in excellent health. Then she remembered her mother's face as they waited at the bus stop. She remembered how tired she looked. She should not have been surprised, but she was. Her mother worked so hard to take care of the family. She was worried about her mother's health. Although she felt guilty, she was just as disappointed about the fact she was going to have to go back home. She was going to be forced to quit school. She was going to have to give up her dreams. She didn't exactly know what she wanted to do or what she wanted to be, but she did know that giving up on her education and going back to the village was not part of her plans. She sat on the edge of her bed. It was dinner time and she wasn't hungry. She knew that she needed to call her father, but she just sat there feeling numb, still hoping this was all another practical joke that Kingasunye had pulled on her.

Ruth pushed her food around on her plate. She had not taken a bite. All she could think about was as soon as dinner was over, she would have to call her father.

"How soon will I have to leave school? " she asked herself.

"What are you talking about?" responded Aleela[9], who was sitting next to her. Ruth had not realized she had actually asked the question out loud. She did not want to talk about it, even with Aleela who was also one of her best friends. Aleela, Kingasunye, and Ruth had been almost inseparable since they first met at the beginning of school. Even though they had only known each other for less than one year, they felt as close as sisters.

"Come on! Tell me what is going on," said Aleela, "I can tell there is something bothering you. You haven't eaten anything on your plate and it's boiled goat. I know this one your favorites."

Ruth looked up from her plate and burst into tears. "I have to call my father. My mother is sick and he says I have to quit school and return to the village to take care of my brothers and sister. I don't know what to do. I feel like my life is over."

Aleela put her arms around Ruth. Kingasunye, who was also sitting with them, jumped up to embrace her upset friend. "We will find some way to help. There must be a solution," insisted Kingasunye. Ruth thanked them and then excused herself to go and call her father. As much as she didn't want to do it, she just wanted to get it over with and accept the inevitable.

"Papa, this is Ruth."

"Hello, endito[10], thank you for calling. You know that your mother is sick," answered Ruth's father.

"Yes, papa. What's wrong?" Ruth asked.

---

[9] Pronounced AH-LEE-LUH. In Swahili, it means "she cries."
[10] Pronounced EN-DEE-TOH. In Maasai, it means "daughter."

"All her strength has left her. She cannot move from her bed. We took her to the clinic and they said she must take some medicines and rest. They don't know how long it will be before she gets better. There is no one to take care of your sister and brothers. You must come home."

"I understand, papa. I am so sorry. When do I need to leave?"

"Someone from the church is helping your mother for a few days. Please let your headmaster know that you must be leaving on Sunday to come home."

"Yes, papa. I will be home on Sunday," Ruth said trying to hold back the tears and not embarrass herself in front of her father.

"Thank you, daughter. I know you love your school, but there is no other way. I promised your mother to send you, but now things have changed. Family must come first."

Ruth pushed the end call button on her mobile phone and stood in silence. She had gone outside to make the call. There were only a few lights shining close to the building so the surrounding grounds of the school were pitch black. She looked at the darkness and her first impulse was just to start walking. She wanted to escape and not deal with the disappointment that reality was bringing her way. It was like someone had taken her dream and thrown it in the rubbish pile. It was unfair.

"Why God?" she yelled. "There must be some way You can fix this." She turned back toward her dorm, not knowing what to do, but knowing she needed her friends.

"He never really wanted me to go to school in the first place," Ruth explained to Kingasunye and Aleela. "He only let me come because my mother insisted. I have never seen her fight with him so fiercely about anything else. But now he has his way. I will go home and be a traditional girl in the village. Who knows, maybe he will even marry me off before you finish the school year!"

Aleela tried to console her by reminding her how she really loved her father and this wasn't his fault. Kingasunye then jumped to her feet.

"Let's pray!" she said enthusiastically. All three of them were Christians, but only Kingasunye participated in the Scripture Union club which was started earlier that year. She was always trying to get the other two girls to go, but it was at the same time as field hockey practice and Ruth was the star player on the team. It was too hard to give that up.

"Fine," Ruth answered. However, by the tone of her voice, it didn't seem like she thought it would make any difference.

"Ok!" said Kingasunye and she prayed a simple prayer, reminding God that he promised to give us the desires of our heart and Ruth's desire was to stay in school. "So we ask that You do a miracle God. We have faith in You. In Jesus' name, amen."

With that, the girls began their evening routine of getting ready for bed. As Ruth put her head on her pillow, still feeling hopeless, she hadn't noticed she had received a new text message on her phone, which was charging at the only outlet across the room where they slept.

CRITICAL ISSUE: FAMILY

For most Kenyans, family is extremely important. However, Kenyan youth are being pulled in two directions when it comes to their family relationships. The old traditions and expectations are facing off against the modern ideas of individualism and independence. Is one right and one wrong? How do we respond when family obligations stand in the way of education?

Family runs deep into the heart of culture. Looking outside of your own culture is always a challenge. We run into a clash of values. Which is more important: the individual or the group? If we view Ruth's dilemma through an individualistic cultural lens, we'll never understand her situation. Another cultural value in the mix is age. In many cultures, the opinions of young people carry no weight. What Ruth wants is irrelevant.

Family was God's idea. The bible speaks over and over again about the importance of healthy families who care for one another. As important as Ruth's education may be, how can she turn her back on her family's needs? It's not an easy situation. Scripture does, in fact, call children to honor and submit to their parents.

Research has shown over and over again that parents are the most important influence in the lives of youth. Scripture Union Africa conducted a massive research project in 2009 and concluded that one of the most significant issues African youth are facing is the breakdown of family.[11] Young people need healthy family relationships. They provide the platform upon which other areas of growth occur.

Again, many issues come crashing together—education, family, work, health, and money. Poverty is like a trap that ensnares the whole family, hindering each of these areas and more. With no margin for error, every time someone in the family faces a difficult situation, the whole family suffers. When the family suffers, opportunities for school or work are lost. Less education means less income. Less income means less margin. Less margin means another significantly difficult situation is lurking around the corner.

[11] Scripture Union Africa. *Report on Big Issues Research 2008-2009*

QUESTIONS

1. In this story, what do you believe is more important: Ruth returning home to care for her family or remaining at boarding school to continue her education? Why do you feel this way?

2. Understanding a culture unlike your own can be difficult. In this type of traditional setting, family needs often come before an education. But, education is a key to better employment which can make a significant impact in reducing poverty. Is it possible for this cycle to come to an end? How?

3. Growing up, what was/is your role within the family? How have you been shaped by the responsibilities given to you? What would have happened if you were focused on other things (like your education or a job) rather than the role within the family?

4. Being the oldest, as well as being a daughter, Ruth is being asked to give up something she desires—her education. Have you had to give up something you valued do to things outside of your control? What has the impact been on your life?

5. You just read that poverty is "like a trap that ensnares the whole family." How do you feel about this statement? Have you or someone you know been impacted by poverty? What were the results?

CHAPTER THREE

Identity

RUTH CLOSED HER BIBLE and put down her pen on her notebook. She looked at the little bird she had drawn and at the phrase, *I have a purpose*, that she had written next to it. She took a deep breath and smiled. That morning, she had woken up earlier than usual. Even though she had slept the whole night through, she felt like she had been up all night. She quietly crossed the room to get her phone which had been charging while she slept. She wanted to check it again and make sure her conversation with her father was not just a nightmare. She picked up her mobile and saw a new message waiting to be read.

"Oh great! More bad news," she said to herself.

She pushed a button on her phone and the first word she saw was "Kidege[12]." She knew instantly who the message was from, even though she didn't have the person's cell number saved in her phone. Only her aunt Naisiae[13], her mother's sister, called

[12] Pronounced KI-DAY-JAY. In Maasai, it means "little bird."
[13] Pronounced NY-SEE-AY. In Maasai, it means "the hardworking one."

her by that name. She quickly read the message. She couldn't believe it. If everyone had not been sleeping, she would have screamed as loud as she could.

The brief message read, "Dearest Kidege, please don't worry. You don't have to come home from school. I will take care of everything. And your father is in agreement."

Ruth ran to the bathroom, where she hoped she wouldn't disturb her sleeping classmates, and jumped up and down. She could not wait until the morning bell rang to wake everyone up. She decided to go ahead and wash up as she waited for her friends.

"I told you. I knew it. I was sure God was going to do something," confidently and loudly stated Kingasunye, who also had a smile stretching as wide as the Rift Valley on her face. It was a combination of being grateful for answered prayer and the relief she felt knowing she was not going to have to say goodbye to her best friend.

"Are you sure it is 100% certain that this will work out?" asked Aleela, "I mean, you said your father never was happy you were here in the first place." Kingasunye cocked her head to the side and gave Aleela an intense stare.

"Don't you say that, sister! I will not allow it! God has done a miracle," she said. And with that said, Kingasunye's smile returned and she let out an intense yell. Everyone at the breakfast table looked to see what was happening and then realized it was Kingasunye. She was always calling attention to herself, but the difference was that today she had a truly special reason.

Ruth's aunt Naisiae was someone Ruth had always looked up to. She was her mother's oldest sister and the only one of the family who didn't live in her village. As the oldest child, she had excelled in school and had been given a scholarship to attend secondary school. It was a program created by an NGO to help promote education among rural Kenyan girls and her aunt had been carefully selected. After graduating, she continued on to university in Nairobi, where she still lived today. She owned her own businesses and was always traveling to interesting places around East Africa to buy and sell her products. When she would visit Ruth's village, she always brought gifts from other countries such as clothes or gadgets she had picked up for her import/export company. For Ruth, it wasn't the money that interested her, because her aunt was not that kind of person. It was the confidence and freedom she had. She was doing what she loved and was good at it. That is why they called her "the hardworking one."

Ruth sent a message to her aunt after classes were over.

"Thank you so much, auntie," texted Ruth, "you can't imagine how much this means to me!"

"Oh, I think I can," responded Naisiae. "Kidege, I am not that old. And when I was your age, there were even fewer opportunities for girls like you. Promise me you will continue to do your best. Remember what I wrote you this morning, 'You have a purpose.' Don't forget that. The next time we see each other, I want you to share with me what you think that purpose is. Start searching for it. Ask God to reveal it to you. Find it and begin to put it into action. I must go now, Kidege. I still have a lot of work to do in order to leave things running while I take care of your family."

"Thank you, auntie. Please know I am so grateful. Please send my greetings to the family. Tell my mother that I am praying for her."

"Goodbye, Kidege. May God bless you and this opportunity He has given you."

As Ruth placed her mobile in her pocket, she went to look for Kingasunye. She knew immediately she had something to tell her. She found Kingasunye outside with Aleela talking with a group of older girls that she didn't know. "Hey, Kingasunye. I think I want to go with you to that Scripture Union club. I love to play field hockey, but it seems like this might be a little more important for me. When do they meet next?"

Kingasunye began to do her happy dance and loudly, as usual, exclaimed, "What great news! Aleela just told me that she wants to go too. It's tomorrow at 4 pm, before dinner. But what about field hockey?"

Ruth tried explained, "Well, I really can't tell you exactly, but I just feel like it's what I should do. That's ok, right?"

Kingasunye cocked her head to the side, made a funny face and answered, "Come on! What do you think? It's better than ok. It's wonderful!"

As Ruth sat in the circle of girls in Scripture Union club the next day, she felt like she had made a good decision. Not only was it another opportunity to spend time with Aleela and Kingasunye, but she really liked the leader of the group, Ms. Nia[14], who was also the English teacher. She really knew a lot about the bible, but she also asked a lot of questions. Most adults that Ruth knew only wanted to tell her things. Ms. Nia was different. It seemed like she actually cared about what Ruth was thinking and feeling. Ruth could tell this was going to be an important place where she could begin to explore what her aunt had challenged her to do—discover her purpose.

---

[14] Pronounced NY-UH. In Swahili, it means "purpose."

CRITICAL ISSUE: IDENTITY

Who am I and why am I here? Have you asked
yourself those questions? The path of self-discovery
and the process of finding our purpose in life are
woven together during our adolescent years. The
development of our identity is a long journey for
most of us, full of twists and turns.

Who am I?
Many would say you are the result of nature and
nurture. Your DNA and the environment in which
you live make you who you are. But we know better.
God is able to do more than we could ever ask or
imagine with our life because his power is at work in
us (Ephesians 3:20).

For Kenyan youth like Ruth, identity is often
determined by your family name, your tribe, your
grades, your language, or any number of key pieces
of your life. Inertia plays its part, even in our
identity. Generations of culture and history push
from behind us, making it hard to deviate from a
seemingly pre-determined path. This is especially
true for the poor and those in limiting social
categories like "girl."

Why am I here?
"You have a purpose." Have you been told that
before? Would it surprise you to know that many

youth around the world have never heard those words? Without an understanding of who we are, we could never hope to discover why we are here. Young people around the world will never know their true identity or understand their real purpose apart from the Gospel.

In Matthew 5:1-11, Jesus describes the identity of Kingdom people. This identity sets us apart from all others in this world. In 1 Peter 2:9-10, Peter proclaims our identity as God's people and royal priests. Paul goes as far as to proclaim that Christ lives in each of God's people (Galatians 2:20). Our identity, our purpose, is wrapped up in Jesus.

Identity is about more than salvation. Yes, we want the youth of Kenya and the world to find grace in God's love. But that's not all. That's not the abundant life Jesus wants for us. When we connect to our true identity, that we are God's masterpieces, we will connect with our true purpose, that God has prepared good work for us to do (Ephesians 2:10).

Ruth—with the help of Christian friends, family, and strong leaders—is walking the path to self-discovery. However, Jesus warned that this path to truth and life is narrow and difficult.

QUESTIONS

1. What do you think the difference is between purpose and identity?
2. How would you answer these questions: Who am I? Why am I here?
3. Ruth's aunt, Naisiae, is a person of influence and a guide in Ruth's life. Was there someone in your life who helped you discover your purpose or identity?
4. How does purpose and identity connect to Jesus' desire for us to have abundant life?
5. Who do you have the opportunity to influence in your life? Is there a young person (or if you are young, a peer) who needs a guide to encourage them?

CHAPTER FOUR

Safety

"PROVERBS 20:5 SAYS, 'The purposes of a person's heart are deep waters, but one who has insight draws them out.'" One of the students in the Scripture Union club was reading out loud. Ruth was scrunching her face, as she always did when she was thinking hard about something. Ms. Nia then asks the whole group a question.

"What do you think is the purpose for which God put you here on this earth?" Kingasunye throws her hand up quickly with an eagerness to answer. "Yes, Kingasunye. What do you think?" responded Ms. Nia.

"I think our purpose is to worship and obey God." Kingasunye spoke with confidence.

"Well, that is certainly true, but I am talking more specifically about you. What is your unique or special purpose? What is the mission that God is calling you to?" asked Ms. Nia, trying to clarify her question.

"I don't know!" blurted out Ruth. Immediately she was embarrassed and looked down. Ms. Nia recognized that this was an important moment and tried to encourage Ruth.

"Thank you so much for being honest, Ruth. The truth is that very few people your age know the answer to that question. It's part of the process of growing up. It's actually one of the 'jobs' you have as a teenager. So I hope that we can all learn more about our purpose this year, as we study God's word and have conversations like this. Next time when we meet, I will tell you my story and how I discovered my purpose."

Ruth held onto every word that Ms. Nia said. She was so inspiring and it was obvious she cared a lot about them.

As they were leaving the classroom where they met for Scripture Union, Ruth leaned over to Kingasunye and whispered in her ear, "Don't you just love Ms. Nia. It would be amazing to be like her when I am older."

Kingasunye put her arm around Ruth and smiled widely, "You already kind of are."

Ruth woke up to Aleela tapping on her shoulder. Still half asleep, she asked Aleela what she wanted.

"Can I get in bed with you? I had a nightmare and I really don't want to be alone," Aleela explained.

"Sure, that's fine," said Ruth and pulled back her covers. Aleela slipped into the bed and pulled the covers up all the way to her chin. It was a chilly night and Ruth didn't mind at all, as they often slept together to stay warm. "Night," said Ruth and dozed back off to sleep.

Ruth had no idea how long she had been sleeping before she was woken again. It was Aleela, but this time was not intentional. As much as Aleela would have liked to not have been noticed, her crying caused her whole body to shake and this disturbed Ruth's slumber.

"What's wrong?" Ruth asked Aleela. Her question was met with only some sniffles. "Let me get you some tissues," said Ruth and he went over to her locker and grabbed something for Aleela to use to wipe her nose and dry her tears. After sitting there for a moment, waiting for Aleela to gather herself, Ruth asked again, "What's wrong?" Aleela took a very deep breath and looked away from Ruth.

"I don't know how to tell you. I'm so embarrassed. I am scared," whispered Aleela while trying not to burst into tears again. Ruth gave Aleela a big hug and assured her that she would still be friends no matter what she told her.

"It's not about a nightmare, is it?" asked Ruth, "Grab your blanket and let's go to the study room and talk so that we don't wake anyone else up." Ruth looked at her phone and saw that it was three a.m. She knew that this was not going to be a short conversation and that she was not going to get much sleep tonight. It was ok, though. She had experience taking care of her younger brothers and sister many times when they were sick during the night. Also, most days when she was at home, she would have to get up very early and walk to fetch water or gather firewood. She was not thinking of herself but about her friend. She knew that something was not right.

Ruth and Aleela snuggled together in the corner of the study room. According to the rules, they were not supposed to be there, but the chance of getting caught was worth the risk to Ruth. Aleela seemed to have more control over her emotions, so Ruth asked her again what was wrong.

"I don't know how to tell you, but I have done something wrong and I am very afraid," confessed Aleela.

"Come on," encouraged Ruth, "you can tell me. I promise that there is nothing that you can't tell me." Aleela stared at the ceiling and began to share with Ruth what had happened.

"You know Mr. Kudanganya[15], right?" asked Aleela.

"Of course I do, he is the new teacher this year. He teaches music and literature. All the girls are always talking about him and how handsome he is," responded Ruth.

"Yes, that's him," continued Aleela, "I have him for a class. He has always been nice to me and a few weeks ago, he asked me to meet him in his classroom after school finished to discuss my essay I had written. When I told the other girls in my class, they were all making rude comments about how lucky I was to be 'chosen' by him. I didn't really know what they meant and thought they were just jealous of me." Ruth was beginning to wonder where this was going and feared that the story did not have a happy ending.

"So," Aleela said and paused. "I went to his classroom like he asked. He was so nice. He told me how smart I was and how beautiful my essay was. He said, 'You are going to be a famous writer in Kenya someday, young lady.'" Ruth was a little confused as she imagined something different. "He

[15] Pronounced KOO-DON-GON-YUH. In Swahili, it means "deceiving."

then told me that he would like to tutor me in writing and I should come by his classroom each Tuesday and he would help me become that famous writer. He said, 'You will make your family proud and earn a lot of money. I am sure of it!'" Aleela stopped talking once more and suddenly looked straight down into her lap. "It was so wonderful. It was like he knew just what I needed to hear. He praised me so much. He even brought me gifts like pens and new notebooks to use to write my stories. I felt so special," said Aleela as she poured out her heart to Ruth.

"Then, just last week, something happened. I was reading him one of my stories and he reached up and touched my arm. He said, 'Your story is beautiful but not as beautiful as you are.' He told me that he had fallen in love with me. He said he wanted to give me everything I need to be a successful writer. He asked me if I wanted him to buy me a computer that I could use to write my first book," revealed Aleela as tears began to form again in her eyes. "Then he touched me again and pulled me toward him. I didn't say anything. I didn't know what to do," Aleela blurted out and buried her face in the blanket sobbing.

Ruth embraced her and after a minute Aleela lifted her head and exclaimed, "I let him have sex with me. I know it was wrong. I was so confused. I thought he cared about me and my writing. When it was over, he was a different person. He rushed me saying, 'Put your clothes back on. And do not tell anyone about this.'"

Ruth embraced Aleela again, this time as if she was trying to heal her friend.

"I am so sorry," she said, trying to console her friend. In her mind, Ruth knew that this was not uncommon. In her heart, she knew this was not right. As she sat there holding her friend, she began to pray out loud, softly asking God for peace, wisdom, and a way forward.

CRITICAL ISSUE: SAFETY

The world is a dangerous place. But when the safety of one person is trampled by the malicious actions of another, we often find ourselves struggling to respond in the face of evil. How could this happen? What will be done? How can we prevent this in the future?

All around the world young people witness adults who abuse others for their own gain. Childish optimism erodes as youth watch corrupt officials take what they want, leaders abuse their power, and average people succumb to the temptation of greed.

When the adults who are designated as protectors, providers, and guides are the very people who prey on young people, who can they trust? A life without trust leads to a life of fear. Fear is a growth inhibitor. We become paralyzed when fear and worry overtake our minds.

A study confirmed that violence against children is a serious problem in Kenya. During childhood, 32% of females and 18% of males experience sexual violence while 66% of females and 73% of males experienced physical violence. Most of these victims will see little if any justice. Beyond that, many will live out the rest of their lives never truly feeling secure and always finding it difficult to trust.

The picture isn't much better when you look at youth safety on a global scale. According to the World Health Organization:

- Worldwide some 200,000 homicides occur among youth 10–29 years of age each year, which is 43% of the total number of homicides globally each year.
- Homicide is the fourth leading cause of death in people aged 10-29 years, and 83% of these homicides involve male victims.
- For each young person killed, many more sustain injuries requiring hospital treatment.
- In one study, from 3–24% of women report that their first sexual experience was forced.
- When it is not fatal, youth violence has a serious, often lifelong, impact on a person's physical, psychological and social functioning.
- Youth violence greatly increases the costs of health, welfare and criminal justice services; reduces productivity; and decreases the value of property.[16]

Because schools are an environment of authority and discipline in Kenya, safety is a serious issue. Students will "submit" to sexual abuse in order to avoid the "punishment" of bad grades. Like Aleela in our story, students are taken advantage of or lead into unsafe scenarios. Victims often avoid reporting these issues out fear of making the teachers or administrators angry. In reality, it is improbable that someone like Aleela would report any incident. Schools perpetuate the problems by caring more

[16] World Health Organization, *Youth Violence Factsheet* (2016)

about their reputations than their students. To make matters even worse, there is a strong culture of blaming women, shaming them into believing they are somehow responsible for the evils they endure.

It has always been the prerogative of the Church to care for "the least of these." We are called to protect the weak and the vulnerable. David Gill wrote,

> *"Where are the Christian men who will stand up and protect these precious women? Where are the fathers and elders who will not only set a personal example of virtuous behavior toward women and girls, but also speak up and act decisively to protect them from attackers and abusers? Where are those who demand an end to violence against women?"*[17]

---

[17] Arthur J. Ammann and David W. Gill, *Women, HIV, & the Church* (2012)

QUESTIONS

1. Ruth was able to support Aleela in a very low moment. When have you had the opportunity to support someone close to you who was dealing with a tragic situation? What was the outcome? Do you think it would have turned out differently if you were not there?

2. Ruth (and King David) cried out to God in a time of suffering. How have you reacted to God in moments of hurt and pain?

3. We believe faith, hope, and love are stronger than fear. Do you believe this? Why or why not? If yes, how is this possible?

4. There were several statistics presented in this chapter. Which one stood out to you the most? Why?

5. How do you feel about the David Gill quote at the end of the chapter? Do you know men in who are standing up for women and girls? What are they doing to make a difference in the world around them?

CHAPTER FIVE

Injustice

"WHAT?" SCREAMED RUTH. "YOU have to be joking with me, Kingasunye!"

Normally it was Kingasunye who was being loud and boisterous, but Ruth could not hold back. "No, I'm not! It's true. And why would I even think about joking about something like this?" exclaimed Kingasunye.

"But I don't understand. She is gone. She left without saying goodbye? How did this happen?" demanded Ruth, a wild look on her face.

"The prefect[18] told me that Aleela had been expelled from school for inappropriate behavior and her parents had come yesterday afternoon to the school and picked her up."

Ruth had been away all day Saturday at a field hockey match at another school about three hours away. She left on Friday afternoon and had gotten back late on the next night. She had gone straight to

---

[18] Prefects are usually "form 3" and "form 4" students (11th and 12th grade) who have demonstrated leadership abilities and help manage other students.

bed as she was exhausted and everyone was already asleep. She couldn't understand how this had taken place so quickly and that Aleela had said nothing to her. She felt hurt. Really, she was angry and concerned for her friend.

After Aleela had confessed this to her, she convinced her to go to the headmaster.

"He took advantage of you. He is a man, you are a girl. That is not right. He should not be allowed to do that as a teacher. You must tell the headmaster," Ruth explained to Aleela. Ruth had offered to go with her, but she refused and said she would be too embarrassed already. So on the day before Ruth left for the field hockey match, Aleela went to meet with the headmaster. After the meeting, Aleela told Ruth it had been a very short and matter of fact meeting. All the headmaster had said was he would get to the bottom of this. That is the last conversation Ruth had with Aleela and now she had been kicked out of school. Yet, nothing had happened to the teacher. She had seen him casually drinking his *chai*[19] earlier in the day, sitting in the sun and reading a book. That made Ruth furious.

"Listen to my prayer, O God, do not ignore my plea; hear me and answer me. My thoughts trouble me and I am distraught,"[20] read Ruth in her bible. She closed her eyes for a moment and thought about Aleela. It had been a week since Aleela left and she still had not heard anything back from her. Ruth had

[19] Kenyan tea is called *chai*.
[20] Psalm 55:1-2

sent Aleela numerous text messages, but she had not gotten even one in return.

Opening her eyes, Ruth continued to read, "Oh, that I had the wings of a dove! I would fly away and be at rest. I would flee far away and stay in the desert; I would hurry to my place of shelter, far from the tempest and storm."[21]

Ruth was still somewhat new to reading the bible on her own. She had always listened to it read at church and sometimes her mother had read her some of the bible stories. However, since going to Scripture Union, she had learned to study the bible similar to how she studied in school. All the girls who attended the club were given a scripture reading plan. Each time they would meet, they would report on how much they had read. Some of the girls didn't take it seriously, but it was very helpful for Ruth. It was always surprising how often she would read the bible and it said exactly what she needed to hear at that time. Suddenly she felt like she needed to do just what David, the psalmist, was doing.

"God, why is this happening? Why did you let Mr. Kudanganya hurt Aleela like that? Are you really listening? Do you really care about us?" Ruth cried out to God and then broke down into tears. She hadn't cried since Aleela left, as her anger was overpowering her, but now she was tired and discouraged. She wanted to know that Aleela was alright. She had so many questions. Had Aleela's father beaten her? There were now rumors floating around that Mr. Kudanganya was HIV positive. Was Aleela infected? Was her friend going to be alright?

---

[21] Psalm 55:6-8

Ruth decided to finish the reading for the day and felt a little better as she read, "Cast your cares on the Lord and he will sustain you; he will never let the righteous be shaken."[22]

It was hard, but she wanted to believe that God would take care of Aleela. As she was closing the bible, her journal slipped from her hands. It opened to the page where she had written, "I have a purpose," and there beside it was the little bird she had drawn. "What is this little bird to do?" she asked herself. "God, what do you want me to do?"

Ruth felt like she couldn't wait until the Scripture Union meeting. As soon as classes ended for the day, she went to find Ms. Nia in her classroom. She had been distracted all day and had hardly paid attention in any of her classes. That was not like her and one of her teachers had approached her and asked if she was feeling okay. Surprisingly, she was feeling much better. There had been no specific resolution to what had happened, but she felt like she finally had some hope that there was a path forward.

When she entered Ms. Nia's classroom, there were two other teachers talking with her. Ms. Nia saw her and asked, "Ruth, how can I help you?" Ruth told her she wanted to talk with her and Ms. Nia said she would be a few more minutes with the other teacher and could Ruth please wait outside. Anxious to speak with Ms. Nia, but with no other choice, Ruth walked outside and slid down the wall to sit near to Ms. Nia's door. She would wait however long it took; this was important. She put on her headphones and listened to some music to try to make the time go by faster.

After what seemed like forever, the other teachers exited the room. Ruth bent over towards the door and peeked inside. Ms. Nia saw her and motioned for Ruth to come into the classroom.

"Have a seat, Ruth," Ms. Nia said and motioned to one of the desks in the front row. "What's going on? How can I help you?" asked her teacher.

"I have an idea and I need your advice," explained Ruth.

"Is this about what happened to Aleela?" Ms. Nia guessed.

"Yes," answered Ruth, "How did you know?"

Ms. Nia explained it was not just students who were talking about this, but some of the teachers were upset about the situation as well.

"So what is your idea and how can I help?" asked Ms. Nia, bringing the conversation back to Ruth's reason for being there.

"I feel like God is telling me to be a voice for change. I was reading in the Psalms and felt God telling me to not just let this happen. I want to gather my fellow students together and talk about how we can do something. I don't know if we can fix what happened to Aleela, but we can try to make sure it doesn't happen again."

Ms. Nia looked proudly at Ruth and affirmed her, "Ruth, you are a bold young lady. And I can see that you are very serious about this. However, I want to warn you. This will not be a popular thing to do. I can tell you right now that the headmaster will not be happy about this."

"I know," said Ruth, "and I have thought about it a lot. I feel like this may be part of my purpose. I just can't let it go."

As they continued to discuss what Ruth should do, Ms. Nia committed to helping Ruth make wise decisions. She was also well aware that she was putting a lot at risk, maybe even her job.

CRITICAL ISSUE: INJUSTICE

How do you introduce yourself?
 "Hi, my name is _____ and I am a teacher."
 "Hi, my name is _____ and I am retired."
 "Hi, my name is _____ and I am an athlete."
 "Hi, my name is _____ and I am _____."

Introductions often involve what we do, what we like, or some aspect of who we are that we want others to know about.

Deuteronomy 32:3-4 says, "I will proclaim the name of the Lord. Oh, praise the greatness of our God! He is the Rock, his works are perfect, and all his ways are just. A faithful God who does no wrong, upright and just is he."

Isaiah 61:8a says, "For I, the Lord, love justice."

God is introduced or described numerous times throughout the scriptures as one who is *just*. In fact, the Hebrew word for justice, *mishpat*, occurs in different forms more than 200 times in the Old Testament. Its most basic meaning is to treat people fairly. Justice matters to God.

We generally think of justice as it pertains to legal matters. Justice means acquitting or punishing a person on the merits of the case, regardless of wealth, ethnicity, or social status. But *mishpat* means more than simply the punishment of wrongdoing. It also means giving people their rights, that is, what they are due. This includes things like love, protection, and basic needs.

When you read the Old Testament, several types of people are continually connected to the word *mishpat*: widows and women, immigrants and refugees, orphans and the poor. In premodern times, these were the sort of people who had no social power. They were oftentimes surviving at a minimum level and any deviation from day-to-day routine could spell disaster. For most of the developing world, this is still reality.

When we see injustice, it should arouse something inside us. When you read about the outcome of Aleela's situation, did you feel her pain? Could you resonate with Ruth's anger? Did your blood boil at the thought of Mr. Kudanganya's evil actions? His actions were not just a violation of a person, but a violation of God's justice, and, therefore, a violation of God himself. God loves and defends those with the least economic and social power, and so should we.

There is a second Hebrew word that helps us to understand the biblical idea of justice. The word is *tzadeqah*, and it typically refers to a life of right relationships. *Tzadeqah* refers to day-to-day living in which a person conducts all relationships in family and society with fairness, generosity, and equity. Throughout Scripture, *mishpat* and *tzadeqah* are linked together more than 30 times.

One final Hebrew word will help us understand not simply what is wrong in any unjust situation, but what God desires instead. The word is *shalom*. Typically translated as peace, *shalom* carries a richer, deeper meaning. *Shalom* is to be complete. It means having peace as well as prosperity, safety, and welfare. *Shalom* is the abundant life Jesus spoke of.

These three words give us a great biblical foundation for our beliefs about justice and should guide us in our response to injustice. Mama always said, "Life ain't fair!" She was right. Injustice isn't fair, but grace isn't fair either. It is only through the unfair and undeserved grace of God, which often comes from the people of God, that we find true *shalom*.

This is what Ruth, Aleela, and every young person on the planet needs—life-giving peace. Youth need peace rooted in love, peace that grows out of a sense of protection, and peace through knowing that their basic needs are being met. Is the church of today willing to be the envoy of peace to global youth?

QUESTIONS

1. There are times in life when things are not fair. Aleela being expelled from school and Mr. Kudanganya keeping his teaching position is one of those times. Unfortunately, these cases are quite common around the world. What thoughts come to mind about this situation? How do you respond to God when "things aren't fair?"

2. Ms. Nia is a great role model for the girls at the school. She affirms Ruth and speaks truth into her life. Youth have incredible potential to do amazing things when affirmed and encouraged. Where have you seen this to be true? In what ways can you affirm and encourage the young people you know?

3. What passages of Scripture give you the assurance that God will act in accordance with His character in times of hardship, confusion, and/or chaos?

4. When you hear the phrase, "God is just," what thoughts come to mind? How can we have faith that God is just in a world full of injustice?

5. Why do you believe the headmaster expelled Aleela but kept Mr. Kudanganya on staff? In a perfect world, the decision should have been much different. As a follower of Jesus, what is our responsibility to fight injustice and protect the "least of these?"

CHAPTER SIX

Voice

"WILL EVERYONE PLEASE SIT down!" insisted Ruth, "We need to get started and we only have one hour."

More than 30 students had shown up to the meeting. Ruth was happy to see that most of the people she had invited had come. She didn't make an official announcement because Ms. Nia thought that might call too much attention to the meeting and the headmaster might have squashed her effort before it even happened.

"Thank you so much for being here tonight. I want to ask, would someone be willing to pray for our time together?"

One of the older girls that she didn't know too well but had seen at Scripture Union volunteered. After the prayer, Ruth began to explain how she felt that God was calling her to be a voice for people like her friend Aleela.

"I don't know what you think about God, but one of the things I have learned this year as I have been studying the bible is that he cares about us and wants to see us treat each other with love and justice."

She could tell her words were resonating with many of the girls. While she shared from her heart, they nodded their heads and gave their full attention. As she retold the story of what happened to Aleela she was careful not to reveal too many details but to focus on the issue.

"The bottom line is that Mr. Kudanganya took advantage of Aleela, a student of his and a minor. What he did was not only wrong but it was an abuse of his position as a teacher, a position of trust. Now she has been expelled and he is still teaching. That is not right and we cannot remain silent," asserted Ruth. No one had ever heard someone speak the way Ruth was speaking in this moment. It was both shocking and inspiring to the other girls. Some stared with wide eyes, some nodded their heads, some looked at their feet in discomfort.

"So what should we do?" shouted Kingasunye. "What can we do?"

One of the senior girls stood up and began to offer some extreme suggestions. "It is obvious the headmaster is not going to give us justice. He prefers to make it all go away silently. I am not okay with that. Mr. Kudanganya should suffer for what he did to Aleela. I think we should take matters into our own hands. He is only one man and we are many. We can demand that he leaves!"

Several of the girls began to murmur and stood up to join the instigator. Kingasunye was right in the middle of the pack. You could see the rage in her eyes. She wanted revenge for what had happened to her friend. Shouting and disagreement began to erupt in different areas of the group.

Ruth stood there paralyzed, not knowing what to do. She empathized with their anger, but this was the last thing that she wanted. This would not solve the problem and she was not ready to see her other friend expelled or worse. This would not be justice, but retaliation. She looked at Ms. Nia and motioned for her to come forward.

"Wait! Everyone, please sit down! Now!" demanded Ruth. She even surprised herself with the way she was suddenly taking control of the chaos that had erupted. The crowd began to take their seats as Ms. Nia made her way to the front of the group. Ruth explained, "I have asked Ms. Nia to come and help us to come us with a good action plan. Ms. Nia, thank you for coming. I know you are taking a risk in being here. Please help us refocus on the issue and come up with some good ideas that can help make sure this never happens again."

"Thank you, Ruth. I would like to ask you all one question," began Ms. Nia. "What is the outcome that you want to see accomplished?"

There was a short silence and then one of the girls replied, "Justice!" That triggered another eruption of ideas.

"We want Aleela back!"

"Answers from the headmaster!"

"Sack Mr. Kudanganya!"

"Payback!"

"No more discrimination because we are girls!"

"Safety at school!"

After the ideas slowed down, Ms. Nia raised her hand in order to quiet the group and get their attention. "I understand what you are saying. I even agree with some of your ideas," commented Ms. Nia, "but how are you going to be able to demand they happen and be successful?"

Kingasunye blurted out, "Well we are right, aren't we? What do you mean anyway?"

"Thank you for your questions, Kingasunye," calmly responded Ms. Nia. "What I mean is that if you march into the headmaster's office and demand that he sack Mr. Kudanganya, do you think he will listen to you?"

"Well he should," protested one of the girls in the group.

"I can tell you that I don't believe he would, even if he should," challenged Ms. Nia. "So you need to decide if you want to create change or respond out of anger."

Ruth saw an opportunity to speak to her fellow classmates again and move them in a positive direction. "I agree with Ms. Nia. I think we need to come up with a plan that will work, not just make us feel better," she suggested. "Ms. Nia, do you have any ideas for us?" asked Ruth.

Ms. Nia opened her bible and read one of her favorite verses, "Don't let anyone look down on you because you are young, but set an example for the believers in speech, in conduct, in love, in faith and in purity."[23] Ms. Nia closed her bible and then asked, "How do you young ladies think this bible verse guides you in this situation?"

The question moved the meeting in a whole different direction. The girls recognized God wanted them to have a voice and they deserved to be respected. However, the biggest revelation for them was that in order to influence the situation at their school, they were going to have to be positive examples. Their language could not be filled with

[23] 1 Timothy 4:12

hate. Resorting to violence or shutting down the school through a protest would not likely bring about the outcome they wanted. So they came up with a plan and asked Ruth to continue leading this new movement.

When Ruth got back to her room, her phone buzzed. "Kidege, it's your auntie. I don't know why, but God prompted me to pray for you just now. I hope that you are doing well. And remember, our Lord has a purpose for you!"

Ruth half-smiled and took a deep breath. She was beginning to realize that more and more each day. There was no doubt in her mind that she was following God's leading, but that didn't mean that it felt any easier. She laid down on her bed and prayed. She asked for blessings for her family, more faith from God that he would guide her next steps, and healing for Aleela. She really wanted to talk with her, but now at least she knew from Ms. Nia that she was ok and her family had accepted her back home.

Ruth closed her eyes and, for the first time in quite a while, fell asleep easily.

CRITICAL ISSUE: VOICE

The American poet Sylvia Plath penned these words:
> *I write only because*
> *There is a voice within me*
> *That will not be still.*[24]

When we talk about having a voice, we mean more than the ability to write or speak words. Our voices reflect who we are. Jesus said, "For the mouth speaks what the heart is full of."[25] Our voices represent passion, purpose, and who we are at our core.

It seems that youth around the world rarely get an opportunity to find or use their voice. Whether because of social barriers, age barriers, or gender barriers, young people around the world are overlooked, pushed aside, or forced into silence. They feel disconnected from what is happening in their communities and powerless to create change. However, history reveals that key movements have often had youth driving the charges of social justice. There is hope for a better future, and we believe it is found in the voices of global youth.

In the 1960s, youth in the southern United States organized and lead segregation protests. In the 1980s, student activists rallied around the issue of

[24] Sylvia Plath. *Letters Home: Correspondence 1950-1963* (1992)
[25] Matthew 12:34b

racial apartheid in South Africa. In the late 2000s in Iran, youth lead demonstrations of over one million people in the streets of Tehran to stand against the government and demand change.

When young people find their voice, positive change is possible. Activism is only one way young people exercise their voices. Think of the impact a powerful voice can have in a close personal relationship. Think of the good a small group of girls could do in a school.

As the church, we must help young people find and use their voices. These voices must be "full of grace, seasoned with salt."[26] It is our responsibility, Church, to equip the next generation to be the voice of truth, justice, and love in the world. Let us not be fearful of unleashing the power of our young people. Let us be their encouragers, their supporters, and, when necessary, the ones who help focus and temper their raw passion. It is so important for the Church to take the time to encourage youth to find their voice. It is equally important for the Church to listen. God has time and again called young people to be agents of change.

The voice of the next generation will be heard. Will it fight its way out just to make noise? Or will we help it to say what the world needs to hear?

---

[26] Colossians 4:6

QUESTIONS

1. Why do you think Ruth decided to speak up?
2. Why is it important to give youth a platform to speak their mind?
3. Following God's leading, or even just going against the cultural norm, isn't always easy. In most stories like this, no one would be willing to speak up. Ruth is about to embrace a difficult task and become an agent of change. What has God called you to do that was challenging? What have you done that went against the norm? What were the results?
4. Has there ever been a time when you have used your voice to be an advocate for others? How?
5. Positive change can take place if youth find their voice. How can you equip young people in your circle of influence to be the voice of truth and love in their world?

CHAPTER SEVEN

Faith

THE NEXT WEEK WAS extremely busy, as all the teachers were giving mid-term exams. There was no time for Ruth to work on her plan or meet with the other girls who had agreed to form a team with her. Early in the morning, when she was doing her devotional time, was the only free space that she had to really think about any next steps. She had come up with several ideas and had written them down in her journal. She wanted to share them with her team and with Ms. Nia, but she needed to talk to her aunt first, who was out of the country on business and not available until after the weekend. It was probably better anyway. Ms. Nia had told her the headmaster had found out about the girls meeting. He wasn't happy, but she had convinced him the girls were not up to anything negative and needed to process what had happened to Aleela. Ms. Nia said he had pointed his finger at her and said, "You make sure it stays that way or you will have to answer for it." Her teacher didn't seem too concerned, but Ruth couldn't bear the thought of not having Ms. Nia by her side and she would make sure they thought very carefully about how they were going to move forward with her plan.

"Kidege, it's so wonderful to hear your precious voice!" enthusiastically exclaimed her aunt when she answered the phone.

"How was your trip to Ghana?" asked Ruth. She loved to hear the stories about the new places her aunt visited. She hoped one day to be able to also visit other places and experience new and exciting things.

"It was very busy and very dusty," explained her aunt. "However, I was able to make some very good business deals. I will begin to import some products made from the shea nut. It is becoming very popular in beauty products. They say it is a miracle for keeping your skin looking young and I am sure it will sell very well in my stores in Nairobi."

Ruth was always impressed with how much her aunt knew and how she was always experimenting with new ideas.

"I also brought you a present, Kidege. I will bring it to you the next time I visit," her aunt told her.

"That's wonderful! I can't wait!" Ruth exclaimed, hoping that she would see her aunt soon. "Auntie, I have something I want to talk to you about. Something has happened here at school and I need your help," continued Ruth. She explained to her aunt about what had happened to Aleela, her friend being expelled and how she had met with the group of girls who wanted to do something about it. Ruth also shared with her about how Ms. Nia had wisely convinced them to avoid doing anything which would have only made the situation worse.

Her aunt was saddened by this. She told Ruth this was not the first time she had heard a story like this. Though things were better than when she was in school, there was still more progress to be made in providing safe and accessible education for girls.

"I am so glad that you feel this way and I want to ask you to help us with something. I would like to invite you and some of the other successful women you know to come to our school and do an assembly," Ruth explained. She described to her aunt the plan she had to have several prominent women come and speak about the importance of finding your purpose. She also wanted them to touch on issues that many girls like her were facing. She suggested a list of topics to her aunt that included mentoring, early marriage, gender discrimination, and sexual assault.

"I know just the right people!" her aunt said. "I will reach out to them in the next few days. When are you hoping to do this event?"

At the end of the semester, there was always an assembly organized by the students. Two of the committee members were in her group and she was sure that they would be excited about the idea.

"I will message you the exact dates tomorrow after I talk with my team. You are going to come, right auntie?"

"I wouldn't miss it for anything and I need to give you your gift anyway," responded her aunt. "Thank you so much, auntie. This is going to be amazing!" added Ruth and said goodbye to her aunt.

It seemed like it had been forever since they last met. They had come a long way from the mass chaos that broke out as they all expressed their anger and frustration about what had happened to Aleela and the lack of justice from the school. Now, they were moving forward with a plan and Ruth was leading her peers towards a positive and God-honoring response. She shared with them about her conversation with her aunt. By then, her aunt had confirmed that three other women would attend.

One of the women was the youngest female elected to the Parliament. She was a good friend of her aunts and they attended the same church. She was passionate about passing new laws which would better protect women's rights in Kenya and she was very excited about coming. Another of the women was a business partner of her aunt's. They often traveled together and her aunt's colleague was often invited to lecture at universities across the country about entrepreneurship. Lastly, her aunt had been able to secure the executive director of an NGO that focused on creating awareness about violence against women and providing services for victims of violence. All of her fellow team members were extremely impressed and knew there was no way the headmaster could resist these distinguished speakers.

They talked about the details of the event. The two committee members who were part of her team took notes and prepared the proposal for the assembly that they would present to the teacher in charge. They also agreed to ask Ms. Nia to be the official moderator for the event. They wanted to honor her and Ruth was just too nervous to try to do it herself, even though the team had suggested she do it.

"I was done accepting the things I could not change. I decided to change the things that I could not accept," stated Dr. Kuria, executive director of the NGO. The room erupted in applause. "I want to challenge you, young ladies, to be change agents. You must stand up for justice. You must strive to live in a society that values a person not because of their gender, their wealth, or their ethnicity, but because they are fearfully and wonderfully made in the image of our Creator."

Dr. Kuria was the last of the speakers. Ruth was ecstatic. The assembly had been even better than she imagined. Her aunt was amazing and the women she invited had provided such a diverse perspective for the more than 1000 students at her school.

Ms. Nia walked to the podium to close the program and she looked at Ruth, who was sitting in the front row.

"I would like to invite one last person stage this afternoon. This event would not have happened with the vision, hard work, and leadership of Ruth Kimeli."

Ruth was not expecting this and was instantly embarrassed. However, she was pushed towards the stage as her fellow classmates gave her a standing ovation. She walked to the stage and her teacher gave her a big hug.

"I am so proud of you," beamed Ms. Nia.

Ruth walked to the podium and thanked everyone for their participation. She looked over where her aunt and the other speakers were seated and thanked them for coming. She was very happy about what they had been able to accomplish. However, she was sad that Aleela was not there to see it. Some things cannot be undone. Ruth scanned the crowd one last time and her eyes fixed on Mr. Kudanganya. She still had trouble looking at him and not feeling hate in her heart.

"This will not happen again, sir," she said in her mind. She knew this would not be the last time she would be involved in an event like this. She felt in her heart that she was discovering her purpose and that God had much more in store for her life. She may be a little bird, but she was not scared to fly.

CRITICAL ISSUE: FAITH

Look at the last paragraph of the story again. What do you notice about Ruth's attitude? Her view of reality? She believes—she knows—she can make a difference. She has faith that things can change. She has faith that God is working in her and through her.

We're told, "The righteous will live by faith."[27] But what is faith and how do we live by it? The author of Hebrews teaches, "Now faith is confidence in what we hope for and assurance about what we do not see."[28]

What is it that someone like Ruth hopes for? What is it that she cannot see, but she is confident is there? What difference does faith make in the life of someone like Ruth?

Even if Ruth's mother and father were both faithful, strong Christians, that faith is not automatically inherited by their daughter. Young people must develop in their faith and understanding of God. It is a process and the goal of that process is for them to think and live like Jesus. But they must be able to do this at their time and in their way. It is our role as the body of Christ to help them walk this road of faith.

[27] Romans 1:17b
[28] Hebrews 11:1

Faith is far too often condensed into spiritual terms. But the faith that Jesus calls us to is much more encompassing than just our prayer time or bible study. Jesus cared for the whole person and called us to embrace faith in all aspects of our lives. Jesus preached sermons, but he also healed physical bodies, fed hungry stomachs, challenged educated minds, diffused complex social situations, and empowered both the elite and the outcast.

We call this holistic ministry and we believe the Church is called to follow Jesus' example of reaching the whole person. If the Church divides spiritual matters from the rest of life, it frustrates a young person's ability to understand how their faith is to be lived out.

Questioning, doubting, discovering. These are all natural steps in the faith development of adolescents. This phase of life is hard enough on its own. Imagine the mental, emotional, and spiritual clash taking place when a teenager faces issues like Ruth did. "Is God just?" "Does God really love me?" "Why doesn't God help me?" "Why does it seem like the bad guys win?"

We set young people up for failure in their faith when we make them believe God doesn't care about their education or their job. There is a beautiful old gospel hymn that illustrates how faith can give us the confidence we need to face life.

Why should I feel discouraged,
Why should the shadows come,
Why should my heart be lonely,
And long for heav'n and home,
When Jesus is my portion?
My constant Friend is He:
His eye is on the sparrow,
And I know He watches me;
His eye is on the sparrow,
And I know He watches me.[29]

This is the faith we wish for the youth of the world. It's a faith that trusts in God's care for their lives, even when facing difficulties.

Hope is an entry point for faith. The church must extend hope in practical, holistic ways, reaching youth where they are. This is crucial to fulfilling the Great Commission[30] of Christ because research shows that nine out of ten people make their decision to follow Jesus before they turn 18-years-old. Reaching youth is not optional for the Church. We must give young people the opportunity to experience hope. Hope, in turn, opens the door for faith in God, and in God's plan for their lives.

---

[29] Martin, Civilla. His Eye Is on the Sparrow (1905)
[30] Matthew 28:18-20

QUESTIONS

1. What components were put into place to make the assembly a success? How might the outcome of the assembly have been different if these components were not included?
2. Did you know that 90% of Christians come to faith before age 18? What do you think this means for the Church? How should we respond to that statistic?
3. In the story so far, who is helping Ruth to develop her faith in God?
4. We've shared that questioning, doubting, and discovering are all natural steps in the faith development of adolescents. Do you believe this to be true? Why or why not?
5. When young people experience hope it opens the door for them to trust God and discover their ultimate purpose and identity. Where have you seen this to be true? What are some ways you can help young people (or your peers if you are young) experience hope?

CHAPTER EIGHT

Now What?

RIGHT NOW, IT'S QUITE possible that you are frustrated, mad, disappointed, or hoping the story you just finished reading would have ended better. You may be wishing that the evil teacher would have been fired or, better yet, sent to prison. Maybe you wanted Aleela to be able to come back to school. Those are all right and just desires. You are not at all wrong in wanting that kind of resolution. However, so many of the problems young people face around the world cannot be fixed in the short-term. Whether it is the political system, the culture, the lack of justice, or poor decisions by the families of the youth that create these issues, most of them require a long-term and systems-based approach. There are more than 1.8 billion young people around the world who need our help. They need us to value them, to listen to them, and to keep their best interest in mind. That is why it is urgent for the Church and the global missions community to recognize youth as one of most strategic focus areas of ministry. Global youth are making life's most important decisions and facing some of the toughest challenges on the planet. They need us by their side as advocates, encouragers, protectors, guides, and mentors.

In this story, we can see three key elements which made it possible for the story to end as well as it did. If the lives of young people are going to be transformed in Kenya, or any other country in the world, then someone needs to be doing these three things in the lives of young people.

First, someone must point youth toward Jesus and a church where they can find love and belonging. In Ruth's story, we first see this in her mother who helped to develop her faith and build a relationship with the church at an early age.

Second, the church and community must provide youth with equipped leaders who can help them discover their purpose and calling. Both Ruth's aunt and Ms. Nia played an important role in Ruth's success and avoidance of some of the pitfalls of her reality. Her aunt helped keep her in school. She also challenged her to see the barriers she was facing as opportunities to explore God's purpose for her life.

Lastly, leaders must invite youth to be part of the solution to their problems and challenges by empowering them to lead and be change agents in their communities. Ms. Nia continued to guide Ruth in discovering her calling and empowered her to address a tragic problem in her school while helping her avoid some big mistakes.

- Jesus and the Church
- Equipped Leaders
- Youth Empowerment

Not only were these three elements important in Ruth's life, but they also impacted her school and her family. When we invest in youth, they have the potential to make an incredibly positive impact on those around them.

The stark reality facing global youth today is that these three elements are rarely all present. Let's take a moment and imagine what would have happened in Ruth's story if these three elements were not present.

LIFE WITHOUT HOPE

A different, but all too common, ending...

Ruth wipes the sweat from her forehead. It's hot and she is feeling it even more now that she is 3 months pregnant. She pauses and stares down at the path in front of her which she walks every day to gather firewood. Last year, at this same time, she was in school. This was not the path she envisioned walking when she dreamed about attending university and traveling the world like her aunt. Every time her aunt would come to the village to visit her mother it would reopen the wound and deepen the bitterness Ruth had in her heart. She was glad her mother was better, but she still felt like it had been unfair for her to leave school and return to the village. She hated her father. He had ruined her life. He had stolen her dreams. And every time she saw her aunt, she was reminded of those lost opportunities and how it contrasted with the reality she despised.

Ruth began to walk again, this time wiping tears from her face instead of sweat. Even though she was married and back with her family, she felt alone.

Just a few months ago, she had received a message from an acquaintance from her boarding school that her dear friend Aleela had committed suicide. The shame of her sexual assault had been too much to handle. While her family had received her back, she was considered damaged goods and no man in her village wanted to marry her. She had hung herself from an acacia tree and her little sister had found her. This hurt Ruth deeply because she thought that if she had been there, if she hadn't been forced to leave school early, maybe she could have helped Aleela. Unfortunately, there was no one in her village to counsel her through it. First, you just didn't talk about things like that. Also, she had lost touch with her other best friend Kingasunye who was always busy with school and field hockey. They had drifted apart because their worlds were so different. This was due in part to the fact that Kingasunye was not hanging with the best crowd. She was involved in a lot of drinking and was sneaking out at night with other girls to meet with boys in town. Ruth had tried to warn her, but Kingasunye was not really interested in her advice from afar. That also hurt Ruth and so they just stopped talking and then stopped texting.

As she walked, she grieved for Aleela and wondered if her friend was better off anyway.

CHAPTER NINE

Conclusion

WE DON'T WANT THIS to be the ending of any young person's story. What about you? We hope you have EMPATHIZED with global youth through reading the story of Ruth, LEARNED facts and information about the reality in which many global youth live, and REFLECTED on how you feel and how it compares to your reality. Up until now, though, all you have been doing has been internal—in your heart and mind. As you finish this book, we would like to suggest three ways you can act.

The first of these is to PRAY. We encourage you to pray for girls in Kenya like Ruth, Aleela, and Kingasunye, as well as youth all around the world. Pray for them as they face challenges. Pray that they would have those three elements in their life—Jesus and the Church, equipped leaders, and empowerment—and that they would experience God's love and transformation.

The second way you can act is to SHARE. Here are a few ways that you could share what you have learned in this book:

- Give a friend a copy of this book.
- Tell the story of Ruth to your friends and ask them some of the questions from this book.
- Suggest to your small group, youth group, or family that you read this book together and discuss it.
- Use social media to share some of the information about the issues that global youth face.
- Write a blog about it or a paper for school/university.

Lastly, we want to urge you to GIVE. This could be your time or the resources that God has given you. Support the efforts of YouthHOPE, Ends of the Earth Cycling, and AfricaHope with a donation or go on a short-term mission project that focuses on youth with New Mission Systems International. You could also begin by volunteering with the youth ministry in your church or by mentoring a young person from your community.

God has given you so much and now you have the opportunity to give back. Remember what Paul writes in 2 Corinthians 9:8, "And God is able to bless you abundantly, so that in all things at all times, having all that you need, you will abound in every good work."

There are so many young people—more than 1.8 billion—around the world that need someone to love them, invest in them, and believe in them. We are challenging you to find one and give of what you have to bless them.

We want to thank you for reading this book. We pray that through utilizing what you've learned, God will do abundantly more than we can ask or imagine in the lives of more youth than we could count.

68707988R00052

Manufactured by Amazon.com
Columbia, SC
29 March 2017